Original title:
Twilight Tales of the Thicket

Copyright © 2025 Creative Arts Management OÜ
All rights reserved.

Author: Jasper Montgomery
ISBN HARDBACK: 978-1-80567-361-3
ISBN PAPERBACK: 978-1-80567-660-7

Tales of Hidden Halls in the Thicket

In the thicket, shadows play,
A squirrel dances, bright as day.
He stumbles on a thistle bush,
And gives it quite the clumsy push.

A rabbit's joke, it bounces low,
Claiming he's the star of the show.
Yet when he trips, with thump and clap,
His ears flop down, a comic map.

The owls hoot, a laugh so grand,
As fireflies glow, they take a stand.
A hedgehog joins, with spiky flair,
Says, "Look at me! I'm sharp everywhere!"

These hidden halls echo with glee,
Where creatures dance, wild and free.
In every nook, a giggle grows,
In this thicket, anything goes!

The Nightingale's Story

There once was a bird who loved to sing,
Her notes would make the whole thicket swing.
But when she slipped on a dewy leaf,
She spun through the air, what a comic brief!

Her friends all giggled, from dusk till dawn,
As she landed on a sleeping fawn.
"Excuse me, dear! I didn't mean to land,
I'm just a singer with no steady plan!"

The fox said, "You've got quite a flair,
To turn a fall into a dramatic affair!"
With a wink and a flourish, she took to the trees,
"This stage is mine, let's chill with the breeze."

Thus nightingales sing, not just for the tune,
But for laughter that brightens the silver moon.
Their stories echo through branches wide,
In this thicket of fun, where joy will abide!

Songs of the Whispering Leaves

In the creaky trees, a squirrel sings,
Bright red acorns, oh what joy it brings.
A croaky frog joins in the dance,
Each note sounds like a clumsy prance.

Breezes laugh as branches sway,
The chatty birds have much to say.
With each rustle, secrets shared,
A giggle here, a wink declared.

Veils of Mist and Memory

Fog drapes low like a silly shawl,
Hiding hedgehogs who trip and fall.
Mice giggle, sneaking past the trees,
While flustered owls croak 'Who'd that be?'

The mushrooms chuckle, all in a row,
Making faces as breezes blow.
In this mystic, blurred delight,
Laughter echoes through the night.

Hushed Secrets of the Sylvan Realm

An armadillo wearing a hat,
Struts through the thicket, oh so fat.
Whispers float on the softest breeze,
As gophers ponder, 'What's lunch, please?'

A secret toad hops with a wink,
While candles flicker, winking pink.
The trees hold tales of giggles past,
In this domain, the fun will last.

Dreams Woven in the Twilight

Kittens play tag through blooming ferns,
While chasing fireflies, this lesson learns:
That nighttime brings the best of cheer,
With giggles echoing, loud and clear.

A raccoon snickers, sneaking snacks,
Stirring mischief in his playful tracks.
As dreams whisper in zany delight,
Laughter twinkles in the soft night light.

Dreams Linger Among the Trees

In the woods, the squirrels argue,
Who can leap from branch to branch?
The owls squawk in laughter,
As raccoons plan their midnight ranch.

Beneath the moon, the shadows dance,
A fox steals berries with a glance.
The rabbits gossip, tails in a twirl,
While fireflies blink, a glowing swirl.

The Solace of Dimming Light

As daylight fades, the jokes unfold,
A badger slips on leaves so bold.
He tumbles down with quite a clatter,
The porcupines all mock and chatter.

Crickets chirp their evening tune,
While turtles race beneath the moon.
A hedgehog snorts with delight,
As shadows play their tricks all night.

Whispers on the Wind beneath the Stars

The mice decide to hold a feast,
But one forgets and brings a beast.
A cat strolls by, so slick and sly,
The mice now dance, their heads held high.

Bats overhead are laughing too,
At the shenanigans that ensue.
The fireflies blink, give signals clear,
While crickets giggle, full of cheer.

Shadows of Many Moons

In the thicket, shadows grow,
A turtle accidentally tows,
His friends around with such great flair,
As laughter echoes through the air.

The nocturnal jokes keep rolling strong,
As owls join in, they sing along.
The hedgehogs snicker, eyes aglow,
In the gentle night, they steal the show.

Flickering Shadows and Muffled Cries

In the gloam, shadows prance,
Scaring critters, what a chance!
A raccoon laughs, a squirrel shrieks,
In the thicket, laughter peaks.

Bats do somersaults overhead,
While owls ponder, cozy in bed.
A fox tries to tell a joke,
But only makes the badger choke.

Crickets chirp in lively tune,
As rabbits hop 'neath the moon.
The night gets wittier, oh what fun!
Underneath the setting sun.

With every flicker and muffled sound,
The forest bursts with laughter around.
In this silly, secret place,
Where shadows play and smiles embrace.

The Awakened Heart of Dusk

When dusk arrives with a silly grin,
All the creatures gather, let the fun begin!
The hedgehog stumbles, trips on a root,
While the porcupine struts in his spiky suit.

Fireflies twinkle like tiny lights,
Pandas dance, claiming their rights.
A turtle joins, thinking it's a race,
But all he wins is a slow, slow pace.

The moon peeks out, gives a wink,
As frogs croak jokes, make us think.
Laughter ripples through the thicket,
As owls hoot, it's the best racket.

In the heart of dusk, the fun ignites,
An orchestra of giggles, moonlit nights.
With every rustle and cheeky song,
In this wacky world, we all belong.

Whispers of the Dusk Grove

In the grove, secrets quietly creep,
A raccoon whispers, "Shh! Don't peep!"
The trees exchange jokes, branches sway,
As the night chuckles at the day.

A hedgehog tells of his latest blunder,
While fireflies flash with orange thunder.
Silly shadows jump in the breeze,
Tickling leaves and wobbly knees.

The brook giggles, splashes about,
"I can't be quiet! What's that about?"
Wispy whispers dance on the air,
As the night wears a mischief glare.

In the dusk grove, laughter takes flight,
With every twinkle, the world feels right.
So gather 'round, in this joyful space,
Where shadows play and smiles embrace.

Shadows Dancing Through the Canopy

Shadows twirl beneath the trees,
Shuffling leaves, they tease with ease.
A chameleon grins, buckles his belt,
In his vibrant camouflage, giggles are felt.

Squirrels leap, throw acorns around,
While a sleepy owl seeks some ground.
"Why so serious?" the shadows say,
"Join our jig, let's laugh and play!"

Moonbeams join with a dazzling sway,
As frogs croak rhymes in their own way.
Each echoed ribbit sparks a cheer,
Filling the night with glee, oh dear!

When shadows dance, no one can pine,
In the canopy, all things align.
So let's sway with the shadows tonight,
In mirthful glee, under starlit light.

Fables of the Fading Day

In a glen where shadows play,
A squirrel stole the sun's last ray.
He wore it like a fancy hat,
And danced with glee upon a mat.

Old owl hooted, 'What a sight!
Is that a bird, or just a light?'
The chipmunks laughed, they couldn't wait,
To join the show, they'd celebrate.

A bear rolled by, with honey's grace,
He missed the nut and lost the race.
They tumbled down – oh what a scene!
The forest laughed; it felt so green.

As dusk approached, with stars in tow,
They toasted marshmallows 'round the glow.
And every critter in the grove,
Declared it night, the best they've wove.

The Forest's Gentle Lament

The trees all whispered soft goodbyes,
As day slipped by in brilliant skies.
A raccoon sighed, 'Where's the moon?
I hope it doesn't sleep till noon.'

The fireflies practiced their bright dance,
While frogs sang songs of romance.
'It's not quite love, but it's real neat!'
Quipped one as he tapped his little feet.

A rabbit trotted with great flair,
Wearing a hat made of sweet air.
He tripped and fell, a sight to see,
The forest chuckled 'What a spree!'

As night drew close, a coyote howled,
'Don't make a fuss, we're all just prowled.'
With giggles shared under the stars,
They dreamed in whispers, near and far.

Night's Silken Veil

The night was dressed in velvet hues,
As hedgehogs sipped on sweet, warm brews.
They clinked their cups and shared a toast,
'Here's to the moon, our lovely ghost!'

An owl dropped in, with a twinkling eye,
'Is this a party? Oh, my oh my!'
A dance was born, with leaps so bright,
The forest spun 'til the dawn's light.

Fireflies joined, their glow like stars,
As raccoons played on silver bars.
They juggled acorns, oh what fun,
Each tumble earned a hearty pun!

But dawn approached with yawns and stretch,
Beetles packed up, their minds to fetch.
With laughter left, they bid adieu,
The night's soft veil, a memory new.

Among the Roots and Reveries

In tangled roots where dreams might bide,
A gopher peeked, with eyes so wide.
He spied a dream of goldfish bright,
'It's dinner time!' he squealed with fright.

A fox with flair, all dressed in red,
Reported, 'You kids, it's time for bed!'
But laughter bubbled from every den,
As whispers grew to a wild din.

A turtle sang of days gone by,
As stars fell down from the silky sky.
'Let's tell a joke!' cried out a hare,
'The last one in is a sneaky bear!'

The forest breathed in giggles' sighs,
With roots that bounced like lively pies.
As dreams took flight and spirits soared,
Among them all, joy's heart was stored.

Enchanted Echoes of Evening

In the woods, a raccoon danced,
A hat so bright, it had them pranced.
Squirrels giggled from the trees,
As the owl winked, "Who needs a tease?"

Crickets chirp a silly tune,
Fireflies flash like tiny balloons.
A fox tried to play hide and seek,
But tripped on a root, oh what a freak!

Bunnies chuckled, tails a'flick,
As the hedgehog outsmarted the trick.
"Join us for a dance!" they said,
While the badger snoozed, dreaming in bed.

A bear did tango, quite the show,
With a parrot squawking, "Go bear, go!"
As the sun dipped down, laughs did linger,
In the thicket, joy danced on fingers.

The Call of the Hidden Path

Through the thicket, a sneaky sound,
A raccoon in search for treasure found.
He hoarded socks, odd and bright,
Claiming them as the finest sight.

Crickets laughed, their voices cheery,
While frogs croaked songs, a bit leery.
"Is that a shoe?" a bunny did question,
Wearing it proudly, his own fashion session.

A hedgehog wandered in a daze,
Lost in a hypnotic leaf maze.
With each step, he'd twirl and spin,
Declaring, "I'm winning!" with a goofy grin.

As the dusk settled, giggles took flight,
In the woods, everything felt just right.
The hidden path, laughter's domain,
Where silliness lived like a sweet refrain.

Lanterns in the Underbrush

Lanterns lit with firefly glow,
Big-footed raccoons, ready to show.
"Step right up! Join our parade,
Best critters here, you've got it made!"

A turtle boasted about his speed,
While a snail said, "I'm the one to lead!"
The hedgehog twirled with spiky flair,
As the owls noticed without a care.

Foxes juggled acorns with ease,
And a ferret slid down the trees.
With laughter echoing all around,
They melted the dark with joy they found.

Underbrush giggled at the sight,
Silly lanterns twinkling bright.
Creatures danced till the stars were spun,
Ending the night with giggles and fun.

Pathways of Dusk's Delights

On the path, a parade began,
With bouncing bunnies and a clumsy man.
Hedgehogs rolled with a squeaky glee,
As the owls hooted, "Look at me!"

Mice in hats strutted around,
They spun and twirled, never fell down.
"Let's have a picnic!" they cheered with pride,
While the armadillo joined in, wide-eyed.

A raccoon brought snacks, quite the feast,
Nuts and berries, laughter increased.
In sunsets' glow, silliness soared,
Each critter's heart with happiness roared.

With dusk in the air, joy did ignite,
Among critters, all felt so light.
Pathways lit by smiles and delight,
Where funny tales weave through the night.

The Enigmatic Nocturne of Branches

In the branches, whispers play,
Squirrels dance in disarray.
Owls gossip, sharing their news,
While raccoons prance in mismatched shoes.

A spider spins a web so fine,
Traps a breeze, but calls it wine.
The moon winks down at the sight,
As shadows chuckle in delight.

Foxes plot with crafty grins,
Making bets on who could win.
A babbling brook joins the fun,
While frogs croak songs under the sun.

Giggles echo through the night,
As fireflies twinkle, pure delight.
In this world where mischief reigns,
Nature laughs, forgets its pains.

Creatures of the Dimmed Glade

In a glade where laughter roams,
Mutts and mice call it their homes.
Bushes rustle, secrets shared,
Each creature dreams, unprepared.

A hedgehog rolls with too much sass,
Claiming it's the king of grass.
While rabbits hop with perfect flair,
Discussing carrots, unaware.

A sleepy bat hangs just for fun,
Chasing dreams 'til day's begun.
Playing tag with the sleepy stars,
Until dawn peeks through the bars.

The chattering crickets form a band,
Jamming tunes on the soft, warm sand.
In the dim, strange wondrous space,
Creatures giggle, finding grace.

A Tapestry of Dusk's Embrace

In the folds of evening's cheer,
Mice weave tales for all to hear.
The grass tickles as they pass,
Swaying gently like a glass.

Fireflies twinkle, match the stars,
As chipmunks banter from afar.
A playful breeze joins in the feast,
Chasing echoes, whining least.

Toads gather round with their drinks,
Sipping on dew while time winks.
They croak of romances gone astray,
In the shadows where whispers sway.

Together they craft a wondrous tale,
Concocting mischief without fail.
In this fabric of night's embrace,
Laughter blooms, a brightened space.

Afterlight's Lullabies

As day drapes in its final light,
Frogs croon soft under the night.
Crickets strum their nightly song,
While hedgehogs hum along, so strong.

Owls hoot in rhythm, oh so sly,
Kittens chase shadows as they fly.
The moon snickers in delight,
While raccoons dance, ready to bite.

Each critter joins in the merry spree,
Lifting spirits, wild and free.
They laugh away the tasks of day,
While the stars twinkle, never gray.

In the hush of night's embrace,
Nature finds its charming grace.
With lullabies woven from cheer,
Every creature holds its dear.

The Murmurs of the Midnight Thicket

Beneath the stars, a squirrel sneaks,
In search of nuts, it loudly squeaks.
A raccoon spills its midnight feast,
Then runs away, the nervous beast.

Fireflies dance in silly loops,
While owls hoot jokes to unsuspecting troops.
The frogs all croak a wild old tune,
Awake the night, let's mimic the moon.

A hedgehog trips on grassy strands,
With little paws, it makes new plans.
The crickets chirp, a laugh to share,
As shadows stretch beyond compare.

Laughter echoes through the trees,
As night unfolds with gentle ease.
In every rustle, jest and glee,
The woods are alive with jubilee.

A Nocturnal Rhapsody

In the moonlight, rabbits prance,
They throw a party, what a dance!
A fox critiques their every move,
While trees sway, in playful groove.

The badgers chat of daily stuff,
While skunks complain their scent is tough.
Hey raccoons, don't you steal my cheese!
They snicker back, 'We do as we please!'

An owl lands awkwardly, a sight!
He hoots a laugh, just to feel right.
Bouncing frogs join in with cheer,
'The night's our stage, it's clear, oh dear!'

Stars twinkle down with smiles so bright,
The nighttime mischief continues in flight.
With every rustle and silly bound,
The laughter of the woods is found.

The Gentle Caress of Dusk

As shadows stretch, a creature tumbles,
The hedgehog grunts, and lightly fumbles.
Silly raccoons sneak on by,
With giggles echoing from nearby.

A bat swoops in, a clumsy mate,
It zigzags wildly—it can't be late!
The rabbits roll in fields of clover,
The dusk is here, they're feeling bolder.

And then a deer with tiny prance,
Gazes upon their silly dance.
The fireflies blink in a bright array,
While night insists, 'Come out to play!'

In this gentle dusk, all creatures meet,
With laughter bright beneath the trees' beat.
Nature's jesters, both big and small,
Share their stories, a banquet for all.

Twilight's Hidden Whispers

With whispers soft, the night unfolds,
As little mice play tricks so bold.
The owls share tales of seasoned lore,
In giggles lost, they can't ignore.

A shadow darts—a chasing game,
The frogs all ribbit, calling names.
"Oh no, here comes that sneaky tail!"
They hide in bushes, without fail.

The moon kicks back, it laughs aloud,
To witness antics of the crowd.
With every rustle and little jump,
The thicket's alive, it's quite the lump!

As laughter rises with the trees,
The crickets play with perfect ease.
In this bright scene of joy and cheer,
The whispers of night bring everyone near.

Whispers of Dusk in the Forest

The sun slips down, a silly prank,
A squirrel giggles, perched on a branch.
The shadows stretch, a playful tease,
As busy bees hum their evening plans.

Owls with glasses, peering down,
Quip about the day's odd sights.
A rabbit hops in mismatched socks,
His carrot friends roll with delight.

The breeze sings soft, a gentle joke,
While fireflies twinkle in a dance.
The creek chuckles, stirs with glee,
As frogs croak out their nightly chants.

With smiles wide and twinkling eyes,
All critters feast in the fading glow.
They swap tall tales, laughter soars,
As night unfolds, a happy show.

Shadows Dance Beneath the Boughs

A bat in sneakers flits around,
Chasing shadows beneath the trees.
The crickets chirp a rhythmic beat,
While a raccoon spills his snacks with ease.

Squirrels pull off the funniest hops,
As shadows sway in a goofy jive.
Mice wear hats and strut with pride,
In this evening's whims, they come alive.

Evening whispers, softly told,
Bring giggles from the leaves that sway.
A hedgehog spins a yarn so bold,
That makes the daisies laugh and play.

With each rustle, a story to tell,
The forest hums with mirth and cheer.
In shadows soft, where laughter dwells,
Life's little jokes bring warmth and leer.

The Evening's Embrace

As dusk unfolds its velvet cloak,
A fox shows off his acrobats.
He spins and twirls to impress a doe,
Who can't help but giggle at that!

The of crickets set the stage,
For fireflies to flash and glow.
A hedgehog attempts a stand-up act,
And stumbles in the after-show.

The moon peeks in, a shy old friend,
Laughing with the stars above.
They kindle sparks in every heart,
A cosmic chuckle, mischievous love.

So gather 'round, the forest's kin,
Under the sky's warm, chuckling hue.
With every gaff and bungle chronicled,
The night weaves joy in every view.

Secrets of the Fading Light

In dim light, secrets softly stir,
A bumblebee with a silly dance.
He fumbles flowers, but no one minds,
In this goofy, bright, twilight chance.

Grasshoppers speak of dreams so wild,
While butterflies gossip, fluttering free.
A turtle shares his slow-motion tale,
Awkward laughs fill the canopy.

With every step, the shadows play,
As wiggly worms tell jokes, half-baked.
A raccoon snickers at his own mistakes,
Embraced by laughter, for goodness' sake.

In whispers low, the night unfolds,
As critters join in mirthful glee.
With every chuckle, a bond grows strong,
In fading light where stories run free.

Chronicles of the Dim-lit Grove

In shadows where critters hide,
A squirrel stole my sandwich wide.
He twirled and danced, what a cheek!
I laughed so hard, I lost my peak.

The owl hooted a silly tune,
While raccoons stirred up a monsoon.
Together they plotted mischief bright,
Their giggles echoed, a comical sight.

A snail claimed he was quite the sprinter,
But slipped on lettuce, what a pointer!
We cheered him on, with utterly glee,
As he crawled home, so sticky and free.

By dawn's light, the jokes took flight,
In the grove where creatures unite.
A caper wrapped in laughter's cheer,
In the dim-lit grove, the fun was here.

Where the Fireflies Gather

The fireflies flicker like disco balls,
They blink and dance at sunset calls.
Beetles clapped their tiny hands,
While mice formed the zaniest bands.

With a grin, the crickets chirped,
A worm elegantly twirled and slurped.
The glowbugs had a glowing race,
Who knew they were such a lively place?

In the midst of this merry show,
A frog took a leap with a not-so-smooth flow.
He landed right on a hornet's nest,
And that was the funniest pesty jest!

As night fell, laughter took flight,
In a world where nothing's quite right.
A gathering of gleeful sights,
Under the stars, in joyful nights.

The Last Breath of Sunbeams

As sunbeams waved their final goodbye,
A lazy cat stretched under the sky.
He yawned wide, ready for dreams,
While bugs plotted their mischievous schemes.

A dog in pursuit of chasing his tail,
Gave up at last, a humorous fail.
"Why chase it?" he barked with a grin,
"Let the tail come to me, let the fun begin!"

Nearby, a hedgehog forgot his spines,
And rolled down a hill through flowers and vines.
He giggled and rolled with a squealy laugh,
Creating quite the bumpy path!

As dusky hues turned soft and light,
The grove chuckled with all its might.
For in its heart, the sunbeams play,
With laughter sprinkled all the way.

Murmurs in the Moonlit Woods

In moonlit woods where whispers cheer,
A raccoon lost his hat, oh dear!
The squirrel chuckled from a high limb,
"No worries, friend, it's quite the whim!"

Owls traded secrets of acorned snacks,
While a fox practiced dance moves and hacks.
With paws on the ground, they twirled with flair,
Creating a spectacle beyond compare.

A confused frog croaked a birthday tune,
Got tackled by a bear in a fluffy, bright moon.
While the critters laughed and shared the tease,
Even the trees swayed in the breeze.

Late night mischief before daylight's claim,
In the woods where giggles became a game.
With secret giggles, and jests that entwine,
The moonlit woods are simply divine!

Nocturnal Cantata among the Trees

Under the moon, the raccoons dance,
Twirling in shadows, oh what a chance!
Squirrels skate on branches with glee,
While owls hoot jokes, as funny as can be.

A porcupine rocks a funky hairdo,
With pinecone beads, it's quite the view!
Fireflies twinkle like disco balls,
As creatures laugh and make silly calls.

The nightingale sings a quirky song,
Echoing laughter, it feels so strong.
A hedgehog juggles apples with flair,
Daring the fox to join the hair.

So in the thicket, where laughter weaves,
A nocturnal party, no one leaves!
With giggles and wiggles, the night winds down,
The best comedy club in our little town!

Night's Whispering Chronicles

In the thick of shadows, whispers play,
A turtle sneezes, the deer say 'Hey!'
A raccoon with glasses reads a book,
Tales of the forest, come take a look!

The owls debate on who's got the best hide,
While rabbits giggle and hop with pride.
With a shake of their tails, they devise a plan,
To prank the old fox, yes, that is the jam!

The badger boasts of his digging skill,
As a mockingbird chirps, "But what's your thrill?"
With chuckles and chuckles, the stories unfold,
Of mishaps and laughter, the night turns bold.

As crickets chirp their sweet serenade,
The woodland creatures make merry parade.
With smiles all around, they share their jest,
A night full of giggles, they love the best!

The Lure of the Lonesome Trail

Down the lonesome trail, a bear meets a bee,
"Do you hum or do you buzz?" says he.
With honey in paw, the bear takes a dip,
And both start to giggle, oh what a trip!

A lost little rabbit still looks for a snack,
Stumbles on mushrooms, 'Oh! What a crack!'
With each funny face that he makes with glee,
Even the mushrooms begin laughing, you see!

A fox joins the fray, with a grin on his face,
"I've got a wild story! It'll set the pace!"
But midway he slips on a fruit left behind,
And all of his wisdom is humor refined.

So wander the trail where the laughter runs free,
Among roots and rocks, there's always a spree.
In the woods where the wild ones meet and bray,
Each step's a delight on this fancy ballet!

Fables in the Flickering Twilight

In the dusk, the chatter begins a new,
As frogs in the pond put on their debut.
A turtle tells tales with a wink of his eye,
While crickets compose, oh, how time does fly!

The dandelions sway to this soft serenade,
As hedgehogs declare, "We're not afraid!"
With thumping and stomping, they dance 'round the lake,

Creating a spectacle, make no mistake!

Even the stars join the fun overhead,
Winking and twinkling as stories are spread.
A beaver with plans on the great big logs,
Says, "Let's build a stage for some funny dogs!"

So revel in fables of laughter and cheer,
Where every creature brings joy near and dear.
In the flickering twilight, mischief prevails,
And the night is alive with comical tales!

The Forest's Echoing Silence

In the woods, the porcupine sneezes,
A chorus of crickets giggle with ease.
The trees shake their branches, oh what a sight,
Even the owls are laughing tonight.

A squirrel lost his acorn, wrapped in a vine,
Chasing shadows like they're made of fine wine.
A raccoon tells jokes that just don't land,
While the skunk considers a career as a band.

All creatures gather, a comedic parade,
As a fox juggles mushrooms in the glade.
But when the moon hides, they fall in a heap,
Snoring so loud, they wake from their sleep.

Enchanted Melodies of the Nocturne

The owl works a tune on his rusty old flute,
While the hedgehogs shimmy in sparkly boots.
A chorus of frogs joins the whimsical beat,
Hopping and croaking in rhythmic repeat.

Bats swing by, adding flip and some flair,
They're caught in a waltz with the bright fireflies' glare.
The raccoon now sings off-key with delight,
While cats roll their eyes in the glow of the night.

The dance gets so wild, the woodpecker slips,
Right into a tangle of vines and some quips.
With laughter erupting, they frolic till dawn,
As dawn's rosy fingers stretch over the lawn.

The Honeyed Hush of Night

In the hush of the night, honey pots roll,
Nectar-loving bears take a sweet little stroll.
But they trip on a root, oh, what a commotion,
Honey spills everywhere, a sticky potion!

A chorus of bees buzzes in glee,
Taunting the bears: "You're stuck like a tree!"
They flap and they flap, trying to flee,
Only to find they've become quite the spree!

The raccoons sneak in for a sugary snack,
Waddling away with a treasure-filled pack.
Laughter erupts as they share the delight,
As the moon chuckles softly, casting its light.

Secrets Among the Mossy Stones

Under the mossy stones, secrets are found,
A turtle in gossip, sprawled out on the ground.
He whispers to lizards in hushed, secret tones,
While snails slowly laugh, making silly groans.

A frog takes a leap, all dressed in a tie,
Appearing so smart, though he's barely dry.
The rabbits all giggle, "What's the big deal?"
But the turtle just sighs, "You don't know how to feel."

The rocks hold their laughter, snug in their beds,
As the night weaves its tales over rambling heads.
With each little chuckle, the forest will sing,
For the laughter of creatures is the best of all things.

Moonlit Murmurs in the Underbrush

In the dark a squirrel danced,
Chasing shadows, looking pranced.
A raccoon giggled, stealing bread,
While fireflies buzzed above his head.

A fox in glasses read a book,
Finding wisdom in every nook.
Chirping crickets joined the fun,
As owls winked at everyone.

A bat wore sunglasses, oh so cool,
Making bats look like the fool.
The night was full of silly sights,
As creatures laughed under the lights.

A hedgehog rolled, a ball of cheer,
Playing tag, spreading good cheer.
In the thicket, jokes abound,
Where laughter echoed all around.

Nightfall's Embrace

A porcupine with tiny shoes,
Tried to dance, but heard the blues.
He tripped and fell, the worst of luck,
But laughed it off, 'Hey, I'm just stuck!'

The owls hooted, wise and loud,
As the badger formed a crowd.
With jigs and hops, they spun and twirled,\nBringing joy to their woodland world.

A deer tried to breakdance, so bold,
But slipped on leaves, oh, the stories told!
Yet laughter rang like sweet chimes,
As the forest sang in joyful rhymes.

In shadows deep, they shared a tale,
Of creatures brave who would never pale.
With every jest and playful scare,
They raised their spirits, filled the air.

Fables from the Forest's Edge

A rabbit cooked a stew so grand,
But spilled it all, oh what a hand!
The tortoise laughed, slow and sly,
'Next time, use a spoon, don't be shy!'

A turtle tried to run a race,
With a waddle-wobble, what a pace!
The crowd erupted in fits of glee,
As the slowest winner there could be.

A wise old owl got lost in thought,
Dreaming of fish, but forgot what he sought.
He turned to ask a passing snake,
'Have you seen my dinner? For goodness' sake!'

With stories woven, quirks and gags,
The woodland friends hoisted up their flags.
In every corner, humor bloomed,
As laughter spread, all sorrow doomed.

The Enchanted Veil of Dusk

A mischievous mouse wore a cap,
And plotted pranks while taking a nap.
He tied up a cat with a funny twist,
While snickering quietly, 'You get the gist?'

A hedgehog brought a funfetti cake,
But the wind blew it right in the lake.
Fish popped up, with icing on fins,
As everyone chuckled, where joy begins.

The moon sneezed, and stars fell down,
An umbrella opened, spun around.
Fireflies giggled and danced with glee,
In a night of whimsy, wild and free.

All around, they shared the fun,
From each strange tale that weighed a ton.
As darkness draped in laughter's cloak,
The woodland burst with every joke.

The Timeless Tales of Wilderness

A raccoon wore a hat so fine,
Strutting 'round like he owned the line.
With a swagger and a jive so grand,
He claimed the forest as his land.

A squirrel tried to steal his crown,
But tripped on acorns and fell down.
The laughter echoed through the trees,
As critters joined in with joyous wheeze.

A deer danced in a feathered boa,
While frogs croaked beats like a free-flowing sofa.
They formed a band beneath the moon,
Chirping tunes that made all swoon.

The raccoon took a bow, quite proud,
As the thicket cheered so loud.
With giggles bouncing through the night,
Wilderness wonders, such pure delight.

Beyond the Knotted Roots

In a glade where shadows play,
A bear tried ballet, much to dismay.
He leaped and twirled, a wobbly sight,
Stumbling over roots, oh what a fright!

A wise old owl hooted a tune,
As rabbits gathered under the moon.
With popcorn tossed and laughter spread,
They cheered for the bear, who danced instead.

A fox donned glasses to read the stars,
While turtles cheered from their tiny cars.
They hosted a ball, with snacks galore,
As critters wiggled, danced, and swore.

Beneath the pines where secrets dwell,
The forest sang its funny spell.
With roots entwined and hearts so gay,
They laughed till dawn kissed night away.

Serenade of the Sable Night

A porcupine played a sweet guitar,
Strumming tunes beneath a shooting star.
His spikes sparkled bright, a sight to see,
As critters gathered round, quite carefree.

A hedgehog sang, his voice so sweet,
While ants marched along, keeping the beat.
The fireflies twinkled like notes in a song,
Creating a dance where all felt strong.

A bath of moonlight wrapped the scene,
As raccoons juggled berries, all so keen.
With giggles and cheers that filled the air,
The woodland stage was beyond compare.

As the night wore on and dreams took flight,
The critters laughed until the light.
With music swirling, hearts were light,
In a symphony of joy, all felt right.

Beneath the Soft Dusk

In a meadow where the daisies sway,
A turtle played cards, but lost the day.
With a grin, he flipped his shell so bright,
While rabbits laughed, oh what a sight!

A badger joined with a pie so round,
Claiming it ancient, a treasure found.
But when he took a bite, oh dear me,
The filling squirted, made quite a spree!

A pair of snakes had a game of tag,
Slithering fast, they tore the rag.
But tripped on roots, oh what a fall,
They laughed and played, embracing it all.

As the dusk wrapped all in gentle wraps,
The woodland critters shared funny mishaps.
With hearts so merry, and spirits anew,
The night whispered secrets, just for the few.

Flickers of Magic in the Dark

In the woods where shadows play,
Squirrels trade tales of the day.
Bouncing logs whisper secrets quite coy,
While owls roll their eyes at a lost baby toy.

Bats perform tricks in the moon's soft gaze,
Chasing fireflies in a sparkly haze.
"Catch me if you can!" the little ones tease,
While frogs croak laughter, swaying with ease.

Mice in tiny shoes dance on the grass,
While the hedgehog snickers from watching them pass.
Each leaf giggles, a rustle or two,
As I join the fun, pondering what to do.

As night wears on, they all start to yawn,
The raccoon announces, "Hey, it's almost dawn!"
With a last wave and a sparkle still bright,
They fade into dreams—what a magical night!

The Lullaby of Starry Nights

Crickets chirp in a rhythmic delight,
As grumpy old owls keep watch in the night.
Fireflies flaunt their glowing parade,
While ants jam out with a wave and a braid.

Beneath the big moon, all creatures convene,
With bunnies moonwalking—oh, what a scene!
The stars nod along, twinkling so bright,
As badgers hold karaoke under the light.

The wind strums branches, a guitar with flair,
While the raccoons whisper, "We've got quite the hair!"
With tinsel and laughter, they sing of their dreams,
The laughter and joy in the night softly beams.

As snores from the hedgehogs echo the tune,
The night stretches on, filled with play and with swoon.
With the sun on the edge of a sleepy debut,
They all close their eyes, wishing for more to pursue!

Gathering of Nature's Spirits

In the clearing where fairies swirl and twirl,
A rabbit in a top hat gives a twinkling whirl.
With mushrooms as seats, the crowd gathers round,
As the woodpecker starts with a comedic sound.

The raccoon's acrobatics steal all the applause,
While the wise old deer nods for laughs without cause.
"Let's hear all the gossip!" squeaks a young jill,
As the frogs hop around, spreading chuckles at will.

Buzzing bees offer cupcakes and tea,
While the turtles contemplate climbing a tree.
With a squawk from a parrot, the party ignites,
As laughter erupts under the magical lights.

With spirits uplifted, they dance 'til the dawn,
As nature rejoices, their laughter not gone.
For in each creature, a tale to ignite,
Is forged in this gathering of joy through the night!

The Enigma of the Evening Glade

In the glade where shadows blend and sway,
A squirrel in spectacles reads out loud each day.
The raccoons in jam jars throw a huge bash,
While fireflies flicker like coins in a stash.

A wise old owl spills secrets with glee,
"Why did the frog hop? To dance like me!"
As the chattering mice nibble on cheese,
They giggle at stories swayed by the breeze.

Overhead, the stars play hide-and-seek,
While ladybugs blush at the kiss from the creek.
The night fills with laughter, lighthearted and free,
In the mystery of oaks, where spirits agree.

As dawn gives a wink to the magical night,
The creatures dissolve in a blossom of light.
With a promise of mischief and fun in their hearts,
They drift into dreams—where every day starts!

The Nighthawk's Tale

In the thicket where shadows leap,
A nighthawk forgot how to sleep.
He flapped in a dance, so absurd and grand,
With his buddies who couldn't quite understand.

They laughed as he tumbled, a sight to behold,
His nightly ballet was comedy gold.
With each clumsy turn, the moon gave a wink,
As he tangled with branches, not wanting to think.

The owls rolled their eyes, 'Oh dear, what a flight!'
'Is that really a bird or a kite in the night?'
But our goofy nighthawk just took a new spin,
In the party of dusk, he was bound to win!

So if you hear laughter from stars up above,
It's the nighthawk you've seen, spreading laughter and love.
In his flight of mischief, he'll never be meek,
For there's joy in his dance, vitality and cheek!

Mystics of the Moonlit Thicket

The crickets were gathered for wisdom that night,
With a glowworm who served as their quirky light.
They puzzled out riddles of love and of fear,
While sipping on dew from a sprightly fern beer.

A raccoon popped in, with a grin on his face,
Claiming he knew how to win any race.
He challenged the starlings, 'Come on, let's see!'
But tripped on a twig, 'It was part of my spree!'

They cackled and chortled, a humorous scene,
As the wise old badger made sure he was seen.
With secrets of forest, he'd nod with a flair,
'It's the fun of the chase, it's the laughter we share!'

So gather your friends, under moonlight so bright,
Find wisdom in folly, and dance in the night.
For in thickets where laughter and mischief collide,
The mystics will chuckle, and joy will abide!

Shadows of Forgotten Lore

In the depths of the night, a squirrel took a leap,
But missed his best branch with a flop and a beep.
The shadows all gasped, then burst into crows,
   'Was that acrobatics or just a bad pose?'

An old fox stood by, with a smirk on his snout,
'There's wisdom in laughter; let's hear it out loud!'
So the creatures imagined wild stories of flight,
Imagining squirrels that soared into the night.

A turtle chimed in, 'I once tried to run!'
But found it most tiresome, at least not much fun.
The crowd rolled in mirth, at the thought of his feat,
While the owl hooted softly, 'Now that's hard to beat!'

Thus shadows revealed not just myths of old,
But the folly of creatures in tales retold.
For among the dark whispers and giggles galore,
The heart of the forest is laughter, not lore!

The Call of the Dusk Wanderer

As twilight began, a wanderer crept,
With brushes of color, the canvas he kept.
A raccoon, a motley, his palette of tricks,
Was painting the world with his quick little flicks.

He bumped into bushes, got tangled in brambles,
Declared with a laugh, 'This here is just gambles!'
From a distance, a skunk sniffed, 'Oh what a sight,
Is he here for the art or a whim of the night?'

With moonbeams reflecting in playful delight,
The wanderer chuckled, 'It's all in the light!'
So he gathered the critters, 'Come join in my quest,
Together we'll make this the quirkiest fest!'

As they danced and they twirled, shadows spun all around,

The dusk painted smiles where laughter abound.
Through the calls of the night, a reminder resounds,
In the heart of the thicket, pure joy is found!

Sylvan Serenades at Sundown

The squirrels dance on branches high,
Chasing shadows as fireflies fly.
A raccoon wears a hat too big,
Looking quite silly, doing a jig.

The owl hoots with a heartfelt cheer,
While frogs croak songs that all can hear.
A fox tries to mimic the tune,
But only howls at the gentle moon.

Bunnies hop with a wiggle and wink,
Sharing secrets when no one thinks.
A hedgehog rolls down a grassy hill,
Turning cartwheels, what a thrill!

Through the thicket, laughter flows,
As nighttime wraps and the mischief grows.
A chorus sung by creatures small,
In the magic hour, they have a ball.

Mysteries of the Woodland Whisper

Beneath the boughs where whispers creep,
A squirrel suspects the owls don't sleep.
He lays a bet with a chipmunk friend,
On who'll catch a snack before the end.

A gopher giggles, with cheeks so round,
Hiding goodies he has found.
The trees seem to chuckle with their leaves,
As the raccoons plot past midnight heaves.

The shadows play tricks, jump and dive,
With every rustle, the forest comes alive.
A dragonfly zooms, so quick and spry,
'Til he bumps a deer—and oh, my, oh my!

As night falls gently, laughter rings,
Through the darkness, the woodland sings.
The quirky critters have tales to unfold,
In the crickets' chorus, their stories told.

Dawn's Prelude in the Whispering Thicket

In morning light, the critters wake,
With sleepy yawns and a morning shake.
The badger hums a silly tune,
While the sun sneaks out to greet the moon.

A hedgehog stumbles, oh what a sight,
Tripping over in morning light.
The butterflies giggle at the clumsy show,
As flowers bloom, they start to grow.

Dewdrops shimmer like diamonds bright,
As laughter echoes, it feels just right.
The briar patch buzzes with games to play,
Where every critter hopes to win the day.

The dawn unfolds with giggles and cheer,
In the thicket, fun is always near.
A merry band on this fresh new scene,
In nature's laughter, all is serene.

Legends Woven in Shade

In the cool shade where secrets hide,
Funny tales of critters abide.
A tortoise brags he's the fastest of all,
While the rabbit just chuckles and starts to sprawl.

A mystery arises from a whisker-twitch,
As a fox plays jokes with a sneaky pitch.
The bees buzz rumors about the bear,
Claims of hot salsa—does he dare?

As shadows stretch with laughter's grace,
Each critter finds their favorite place.
A chipmunk juggles acorns with glee,
While the owls watch with rapt curiosity.

In this realm of playful delight,
The legends of shade come alive at night.
Every whisper a story, every laugh a tale,
In the heart of the forest, merriment prevails!

Whimsy at Dusk's Door

As shadows stretch their eager arms,
The squirrels dance with tiny charms.
A raccoon dons a feathered hat,
While fireflies glow, 'Look at that!'

The moon peeks through, a cheeky grin,
The owls hoot softly, 'Where'd you bin?'
A fox in socks rehearses lines,
In search of snacks and old moonshrines.

A badger juggles acorns round,
While hedgehogs spin, without a sound.
The night is young, the fun's begun,
In this wild world where all is undone.

With laughter shared by critters bright,
They celebrate the playful night.
Amid the giggles and the cheer,
The magic grows as friends draw near.

The Secrets of the Canopy Veil

The boughs overhead whisper low,
'There's mischief here, just so you know!'
A squirrel slips, a plunge, a 'whoops!',
While laughter echoes from the troops.

A caterpillar's conga line,
In band of bugs, they twirl and twine.
A chattering crow calls out a game,
Of hide-and-seek, oh, what a fame!

Giggling shadows in leafy lanes,
With ticklish grass and playful gains.
In this canopy, secrets thrive,
Where all it takes is joy to thrive.

As dusk unfolds its silken thread,
The secrets stir, and laughter spreads.
In merry tunes, the thicket thrives,
A wondrous world where joy survives.

Echoes of Enchantment in the Twilight

Beneath the stars, a band of mice,
Hold court with giggles, oh so nice.
A hedgehog wears a crown of leaves,
While all around, the thicket heaves.

The wind it whistles, a playful tease,
As rabbits dance with utmost ease.
A curious crow tries on a shoe,
And asks the ants for fashion too.

A glowworm flickers with a wink,
Calling friends to join and link.
In this realm where whimsy flows,
Magic blooms, and laughter grows.

As night advances with a sigh,
The fireflies wish their dreams to fly.
Echoes of joy through branches sway,
In this delightful, wacky play.

The Murmuring Thicket's Heart

In the thicket's pulse, a giggly hum,
Where a goose plays drums, and ants do jump.
A party starts beneath the moon,
With every critter singing a tune.

The bushes sway with hidden glee,
As rabbits serve up herbal tea.
A raccoon brings his scrapbook tales,
Of daring deeds and great chivalres.

A whispering breeze joins the fun,
While chameleons dress for a run.
The heartbeat of this merry grove,
Is laughter, making joy to rove.

As night descends, the critters cheer,
Creating memories they hold dear.
In thicket's heart, the spirit's light,
Keeps secrets safe till morning's bright.

www.ingramcontent.com/pod-product-compliance
Lightning Source LLC
Chambersburg PA
CBHW072137200426
43209CB00050B/70